BREAKING
THE
BRAIN CODE

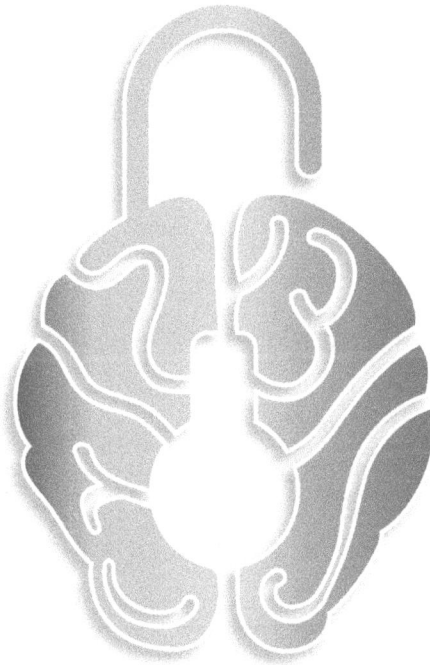

Easy Lessons for Your
Network Marketing Career

KEITH & TOM "BIG AL" SCHREITER

Breaking the Brain Code

© 2021 by Keith & Tom "Big Al" Schreiter

Published by Fortune Network Publishing

PO Box 890084

Houston, TX 77289 USA

Telephone: +1 (281) 280-9800

BigAlBooks.com

ISBN-13: 978-1-948197-93-9

CONTENTS

PREFACE

"Yes! I want success! I am 'all in' on my journey to the top!"

Our brain listens to our optimistic pep talk, and then ignores it. What???

"This time it will be different. I will work on my New Year's goal every day until I reach it."

Our brain listens, acknowledges our good intentions, and laughs. Then it orders another beer and some popcorn, leans back, and watches the fantasy.

"I am a winner! I have the power within me! I will succeed!"

Our brain listens and thinks, "Sounds like some overpriced motivational weekend cult." And then our brain goes back to working full-time to sabotage our success. What is that all about?

Our brains are ... messed up!

Our prospects' brains are messed up too!

We have deep subconscious mind programs that tell our brains what to do.

Our brains are survival organs designed to keep us alive. And if we are reading this right now, our brains have done a pretty good job so far.

Let's think about this. The main mission of our brains is to keep us alive. Brains are perfectly designed to keep us out of danger, to avoid predators, and to survive.

Our brains are not designed for network marketing. Our prospects' brains suffer the same deficiency.

What does this mean? Because our brains have a different mission, our decisions don't support our network marketing daily actions. And it gets worse. Our brains work against us much of the time. The result? Frustration and poor results.

What can we do? Trick our brains. Yes, we will have to work around our brain limitations to get the network marketing results we want.

What about our prospects' brains? Are they closed-minded? Do they prevent new, helpful information and choices? Yes.

Do our prospects' minds suffer from confirmation bias? Fear of change? Processing errors?

Yes. Our minds suffer from all these things, but we don't want to admit it. We can help our prospects overcome their mind limitations by understanding basic brain rules.

Think of brain rules like this.

Imagine we have poor vision. We can't see clearly.

Brain rules are like putting on a pair of corrective glasses. These glasses allow us to see what we couldn't see before. Brain rules may not change how our brains work, but they will allow us to overcome the handicap of inaccurate vision.

Let's use brain rules so everyone can change for the better.

The good news?

This isn't a textbook on brain science. We won't have to learn about neurons, dendrites, neural nodes, and synapses. No biology or psychology books were harmed in the writing of this book.

Instead, we will focus on practical rules to help us control our brains, and to help us talk to our prospects' brains more effectively.

THERE ARE TWO YOUNG MEN.

They are in the same company.

They have the same incredible products.

They offer the same outstanding opportunity.

They live in the same city.

They have the same prospects.

They experience the same weather.

They operate in the same economy.

Yet one young man struggles, while the second young man succeeds. Why?

The first young man says, "I will talk to everyone. With incredible products and an outstanding opportunity, prospects will want to join."

What happens? The prospects procrastinate, some say they are not interested, and many refuse to listen. His obvious reaction? "Blame the universe!"

The second young man says, "Prospects will love my incredible products and outstanding opportunity, if they open their minds and hear my message. How can I get them to listen? How can I get them to open their minds? How can I deliver my message in a way that they will appreciate?"

The second young man knows that human brains are not logical. Human brains make snap judgments, horrible decisions, fall prey to irrational prejudices, and seldom listen. Even if the products and opportunity are great, it won't matter if prospects won't listen to him or believe him.

The second young man learns basic brain rules so that his message can be effective. And that is all we ask. We want our prospects to hear our message without prejudice. Then they can decide if our message will serve them or not.

We must do more than read or memorize great facts. We have to find a way to get our message inside our prospects' heads.

DO PROSPECTS' EARS REALLY WORK?

Do prospects' ears actually work, or are they just for show?

Here is the "no" conversation that plagued my early career.

When I started network marketing 50 years ago, I wanted to be "Master of the Universe." This was my chance to get paid what I was worth.

And yes, I got paid exactly what I was worth. Zero!

With the confidence that comes with ignorance, and a bit of amateur pride, the universe overpaid me by allowing me to earn zero. I assumed that network marketing was the only profession in the universe that didn't require skills. That was a dumb assumption.

My conversations with prospects went something like this:

Me: "Hi."

Prospect: "No."

Me: "My name is Big Al."

Prospect: "No."

Me: "But don't you want to--"

Prospect: "No."

Me: "Well, can I at least tell you--"

Prospect: "No."

How do amateur network marketers explain this? They don't. They shrug their shoulders and say, "We are victims. Prospects are stupid. We'll talk to someone else."

That is why there is a difference between amateur network marketers and professional network marketers.

We can choose which group we want to be in.

The "insiders," the professional network marketers, learn brain rules. What are brain rules?

These are shortcuts and tools that we use to control our brains. We want our brains to work for us, and not against us.

We can use these same shortcuts and tools to get our message past our prospects' natural brain defenses. Now our prospects hear our message. And isn't that what we want? For our prospects to actually hear our message? To be able to give them one more option to improve their lives?

It doesn't matter how wonderful our company video or presentation is ... if no one will look at it. We can't help people if we can't get through to them.

Want an example of one of these brain rules?

See if this is useful.

Brain rule: "People don't want to change their minds."

Does that sound familiar?

If we change our minds, we feel that we were wrong. Nobody wants to feel wrong. Plus, we have a strong bias against information that disagrees with our current beliefs. This is why we defend our favorite band or sports team; it's called confirmation bias.

What is the solution? What if we want open-minded prospects who will say "yes" to our message? Simple!

If prospects don't want to change their minds, then open with a question that has the "yes" answer we want.

Example #1: "Would you want to look at my part-time business?" (We can expect a negative reply.)

Example #2: "Do you hate commuting to work every day?" (Our odds of a "yes" reply are good. Our prospects don't have to change their minds to say "yes" to our question.)

Amateur network marketers who follow example #1 can expect massive rejection and no business.

Professional network marketers who follow example #2 will have lots of prospects to talk to.

This looks like fun. Before we move on, let's do a few more examples of asking the right questions. Ready?

Example #1: "Can I give you a presentation on how you can get rich?"

Example #2: "My neighbor is earning a lot of extra money. Would you like to know how he is doing it?"

Obviously, Example #2 will get more prospects to listen.

Example #1: "Call your friends and relatives. Tell them how good our products and opportunity will be for them. Okay?" (Ugh, we can feel the resistance already.)

Example #2: "Make sure to let your friends and relatives know first. You don't want them to think you didn't like them and wouldn't even give them a chance. We don't want to be embarrassed, do we?"

Example #2 feels better, doesn't it?

Brain rules are not hard to learn. But if we don't know brain rules, we will be victims for the rest of our careers.

We will struggle to find prospects, struggle to hold our prospects' attention, and go bald from scratching our heads wondering why prospects don't connect with us. Now that is an ugly career.

Top marketers use brain rules to communicate with us all the time. That is why we hear their messages. And that is how we decide if their message will serve us or not. We should give the same courtesy to our prospects.

Let's take a look at another example of re-wording our message.

Imagine a salesman, who wants to help us save money by switching our utility service to his company, tells us:

"I want you to change your utility services to my company."

Change? No, not for us. We don't know this salesman. Our minds think, "What if the electricity fails in a storm? Would this new company fix the problem? What if we won't save money, or there is some other trick? Will the new company drain out my old electricity and replace it with lower voltage that won't work?"

A little re-wording could make a huge difference for our brains. Now imagine the salesman said:

"It takes a lot of time and effort to save money on our bills. But we can reduce our bill in only 4 minutes."

Bam!

These words made it easier for us to open our minds, lower our prejudices, and add one more option for our lives.

We have two choices for our career:

Choice #1: Watch our conversations bounce off our prospects' foreheads, shatter on the floor, and then complain, "Life isn't fair! No one wants to listen." (Yes, this is a strategy, but it's a poor strategy. Yet many amateur networkers use it!)

Choice #2: Learn some brain rules. Become a professional network marketer. Feel the power. Watch prospects listen. Get the bonus checks we deserve.

MATH!

Our brains haven't changed much since Neanderthal times. We were bad at math then, and … we still are bad at math.

As a survival organ, the brain has more important things to do than math. We don't inherit math. It is a learned skill. Something extra. Most people ignore the "extra" and get on with their lives.

While there are math nerds like me, most people will cringe at the following examples.

- "If a 14-ounce bottle of ketchup is $10.68, would a 680 ml bottle at $17 be a better value?"
- "We have 11% more patents than our closest competitor."
- "Over 62% of our users give us a five-star review."
- "You earn 6% of the unencumbered volume past your first Diamond leg."
- "3% of gross sales go into the global bonus pool, and are split up proportionately to the amount of qualifying shares."
- "So you earn 18% when your group volume is over 7,000 points. Isn't that great?"
- "To qualify for the fast-start bonus, you must sponsor 3 people who each have two qualified legs."

Do we feel the fog advancing over our brains? We zone out, and then wait for something simpler to listen to.

Are we saying that our math facts should be ignored?

Yes.

Math is too tedious for most humans to process.

If we insist that we have to explain our wonderful math concepts, how about making them easier to understand? Some examples:

Before: "You need $1,000 in volume to qualify."

After: "You need about 10 customers."

Before: "Our higher-quality product is only 31% more expensive than the cheap, low-quality stuff at the store."

After: "You can have something that works, or you can have junk."

Before: "He is a six-figure earner, and has only worked this business part-time for 13 months."

After: "Does he look special or overly-talented? No. And yet after only one year, he's earning $2,000 checks every week."

Before: "All of our autoshipments save 15% off the retail price. You will be a preferred customer."

After: "Like saving money? Have this shipped automatically every month, and put an extra $20 in your pocket."

When most of our prospects hear math, they turn off their minds.

That means we talk, but no one is listening. Wouldn't that be a recipe for disaster?

Still skeptical about numbers?

Prospects won't take the time to memorize numbers from a salesman.

Let's prove it to ourselves that our minds are terrible at memorizing numbers. Ready?

Memorize the following ten numbers.

1. 174

2. 2,091

3. 71.4

4. 954

5. 219.5

6. 102,008

7. 34

8. 2,018

9. 82

10. 17

If we are like most people, we won't even try. We know it is too hard for our brains. We decide to skip trying this so that we can do something else with our limited brain power.

Our world has infinite data that we could memorize. Unfortunately, our brain power is limited. We will only notice the data that is important to us. And of what we notice, we will only make the effort to memorize a tiny percentage.

Our brains developed tens of thousands of years before network marketing compensation plans. There is a mis-match.

Our data-rich, number-rich presentations will be ignored and forgotten. Let's save our time, and our prospects' time.

Still skeptical?

Here is a great example of how our minds simplify numbers with instant shortcuts.

"If it is more expensive, it must be higher-quality."

Is this always true? No!

But it is often true. And that is enough for our brains to say, "Uh, close enough. Let's not think too hard here. Let's move on to the next thing."

This is the default option for our brains: "So much to do, so little time. Let's make an instant judgment and move on to the next item. No time for math brain-twisters."

WHAT DO OUR BRAINS DO EVERY DAY?

They predict. They are prediction machines.

Brains get stuck in a dark space inside our heads. They try to figure out what is in the unknown world outside of our heads. Our brain gets hints about what is outside.

- Smell. That is a clue.
- Hearing. That helps a lot.
- Touch. Very nice.
- Taste. Interesting.
- And ... vision!

Now before we get too excited about vision, let's see how much vision actually helps our brains.

Take a toilet paper roll. Throw away the toilet paper. Keep the little cardboard tube in the center.

Place the little cardboard tube up to one eye as if it were a telescope. Close our other eye. Walk around a bit observing the world through this very narrow cardboard tube. That gives us some idea of how little our brain actually sees of the outside world.

There are too many details in our vision for our brain to record or pay attention to. Our brain makes a decision. It says, "I only will focus on a little bit. Most of the stuff my eyes see is normal. I have seen it before. I will ignore almost everything. I will use my limited focus to watch for danger, and notice things that are different."

Yes, most things our eyes see never get recorded into our brains. These things were not important.

Our brains take our limited vision and our other four senses, and attempt to figure out what is happening outside of our heads. Not very pretty.

Let's prove this to ourselves.

Let's say that we walked to the store yesterday. Did we notice everything that happened on the left and right as we walked? No. Do we remember the details of every car that passed by while walking? No. Do we remember the prices of store items we didn't buy? No.

Last week we attended a party. 30 people introduced themselves to us. How many of their names do we remember?

We listen to a one-hour lecture. Later, when we arrive home, our spouse says, "Tell me all about the lecture." After two minutes, we run out of things to say. It appears 58 minutes of the lecture was never recorded into our brains.

Our brains are not video recorders. Our brains take little bits and pieces that seem important, and work with these bits. Sometimes we record some of this to our memories. The rest? Forgotten!

Even our memories are messed up. Our brains do not completely record the actual memory. It only saves bits. When we recall a memory, it is our brains reconstructing a general representation based upon the little pieces we remember.

So our memories are not accurate??

No, our brains get our memories semi-accurate. Brains have to make up a lot of stuff to fill in the gaps.

Here is an example of a messed-up memory.

When I was three years old, I sat on a bench at the dining table of my grandparents' home. They had 10 children. I can see this memory clearly in my mind. Perfect.

I can see myself sitting there between two of my uncles.

Wait! That is not possible.

How can I see myself sitting between two of my uncles? That would mean I would be sitting on the other side of the table looking at me. Uh-oh. This couldn't have happened the way I remember. My mind made it up based upon the bits it remembered.

And this memory is a "maybe" at best. At three years old, our brains are still trying to figure out how to make memories. That could explain why we don't remember much of what happened before age five.

Our minds are messed up.

This is why we use brain tricks to overcome our brains' shortcomings.

This brings us back to prediction.

Imagine our brains sitting inside our heads. What should our brains be doing?

The #1 brain job is to keep us alive. To protect us from danger.

Our brains look at the input from our five senses, and try to predict what is going to happen NEXT.

Our brains are prediction machines. Our brains guess what will happen next so it can be prepared to keep us alive. Some examples?

Imagine we are sound asleep. We wake up, jump to our feet, and then feel like we're going to faint. What happened? We need more blood pressure standing up. Our brain did not have enough time to tell the rest of our body to pump up the blood pressure. Our brains don't like messing up like this.

We hear a rustling in the bushes next to us. Our brains say, "That could be a predator. Walk further away from that bush quickly."

We play basketball. We see the basketball bounce off the rim, and our brain makes a prediction where that basketball will go. Then, our brain tells us to move to the predicted location.

We trip and start falling into the lake. Our brain thinks, "It is going to be wet very soon. Breathing will be a problem underwater. Grab a quick breath and then close our mouth and nose." A great job of survival prediction.

So is this what the brain does all day?

Pretty much. Our brains don't spend a lot of time or effort on the secrets of the universe. Our brains have a job to do, to keep us alive.

PREDICTION SKILLS.

We talk. Our audience appears to listen. However, we are professionals. We know better. Their eyes are open, they gently nod in agreement, but we know they are not listening. Nothing gets recorded.

Too much information. Blank stares. Nothing feels important to our audience. What are their brains predicting?

"This salesman is going to talk forever. More meaningless facts that I would forget about anyway. I will hear that things are wonderful, this is the best, something everyone needs, and blah, blah, blah. Yawn. Oh look! That lady has green hair! I never see that in my neighborhood."

If we want to get our audience's attention, we need to break their prediction accuracy. How do we do that? With a surprise.

Have we ever listened to a comedian? How do comedians keep their audience engaged? With surprise. Surprise makes good comedy. We predict an ending to the comedian's story, but our prediction turns out wrong. This keeps us engaged. Listen to a stand-up comedian and notice how often there is a surprise ending to the humor.

Can we surprise our audience? Yes.

Are we naturally good at this? Not likely. We will get better in the future now that we know surprise holds attention.

So what can we do in the meantime to get our audience's attention?

Ask questions!

Imagine we have an amazing fact. We could simply tell our audience the fact, but they might forget it quickly. Too risky.

Instead, we will ask a question. Now we have our audience's attention. They have to pay attention as they try to guess the answer to our question. And if our answer is absolutely amazing, they will be surprised. Ka-ching! We succeed in getting one little piece of information into our audience's brains. Whew! That was a lot of work, but we are professionals. We can do this.

Ready for some examples?

Question to the audience: "Consider your 10 closest neighbors. How many of them get overcharged on their electric bills?"

The audience pauses to think. "I don't know? Two? Four? I wonder what is the correct answer?"

Us: "9 out of 10 electricity bills in our neighborhood get overcharged. That is money stolen directly from our pockets."

An amazing fact. And we got it inside our audience's brains! We are good.

Here is another example.

Question to the audience: "At what age does our skin begin to wrinkle? 25? 30? 35? 40?"

Our audience mumbles, looks at their partner's wrinkles. They think, "I have to make a guess here."

We have our audience's attention!

Then we announce the answer, "Age 23!"

The audience gasps. There are looks of horror across their faces as they think, "I hope you have a solution!"

This is too easy. Let's do another example.

Question to the audience: "There are 10 people in your row. Look at them for a second or two. How many of them do you think have a calcium deficiency?"

The audience didn't expect this question. Plus, now they must look at everyone in their row. Some look healthy, and others, well, maybe they could have a calcium deficiency that ruined their looks.

Us: "68% of the people in your row have a calcium deficiency! Staggering!"

Shocking? Does this get our audience's attention?

But wait! We messed up. We used math. Now, that was dumb.

What does the number 68% mean to most people? Not much. It seems to mean a lot, but they're not sure. We missed our chance.

Let's redo our question and make our math work for us, instead of against us.

Question to the audience: "Two out of three people have a calcium deficiency in this country. Look at the person on your right and the person on your left. Guess which two of you have that deficiency. If only one of your neighbors looks okay, then you are one of the calcium losers."

Now this is getting interesting. Let's do one more example for opportunity.

Question to the audience: "You have an average income of $52,000 a year. Banks are paying 3% interest. If you sacrificed your family life and turned your 8-hour days into 9-hour days at work, how much extra would you have at the end of 20 years?"

The audience stares into space. "Oh no! Math! Turn off my brain! Well, if I give up my family for 20 years, I will only see my kids on weekends. Ouch. This better be at least a million dollars!"

Us: "Got a number in your mind? How large is your number? I know you are thinking it better be worth it, as you love your family. Well, here's the answer. In 20 years you would have about $168,000 after taxes. That is before inflation. In 20 years, that could be the average car price. Yes, we sacrificed our lives for a ... car. Would you like to know a better way?"

The audience is thinking, "I am not going to trade my family for a car!" We have the audience's attention. This is not what their minds predicted.

Yes, with this simple question technique, we can take responsibility if our message is heard or not. We don't have to blame prospects anymore.

And what if we decide not to do this? That means we decide to withhold our offer or opportunity from our prospects. That is selfish. We don't want to be that kind of person.

Breaking the pattern.

Our prospects' brains predict what will happen next. When the prediction is wrong, they pay attention.

An example?

During my fattest days, this was so much fun. I would approach the hotel receptionist or reservation agent at the airport, and say, "Hi."

Their minds predicted this. I was one more boring customer for them to process. Very little chance of an upgrade or helpful advice.

And what was their automatic response to my greeting?

"Hello. How are you today?"

My response? "Fat. Just like yesterday."

Their automatic response? "Great. And how can I help you today? … Uh, uh wait. What did you say?"

"Fat. Just like yesterday." And they smile. They didn't predict that response.

And now I have someone listening who will pay attention to what I say next.

Too easy?

Yes. We know our prospects' brains will remain in a bored, comatose mode unless something unpredictable happens. This all makes sense. We can do this anytime we want.

What happens if we are too predictable?

Our prospects' brains ignore us. Their brains think, "Nothing new here. Move on. Find something more interesting."

Now our prospects check their phones for messages. They think about last night's movie. They ignore us while waiting for our boring conversation to finish.

HOW TO TURN ON OUR IMAGINATIONS.

"Nothing good ever happens to me."

"That is easy for others, but not for me."

"You can't teach an old dog new tricks. I am old."

"Why try when I will only fail?"

"Some people have all the luck!"

"I never get a break."

It is easy to fall into this mindset. Our brains want to protect us from disappointment.

It is easy to have these programs. Hopefully we suppress them. But our prospects? Oh my! They might live by these programs. This can be a challenge.

How do we overcome our prospects' negative programs? Easy. Here are some phrases that will do just that.

"Imagine that ..."

We can command someone's brain to leave the current reality and to imagine something in the future.

Here are some examples.

- "Imagine that you had an extra $500 a month."
- "Imagine you did not have to go to work five days every week."

- "Imagine that we could build this business together and take our families on a luxury holiday."

- "Imagine that your next electricity bill was $20 lower."

- "Imagine you had energy all afternoon."

- "Imagine that our skin could get younger while we sleep."

- "Imagine for a moment that this business did work for you. What would you do then?"

It is easy to transport our prospects and ourselves into a more positive future. Yes, we can use these words on ourselves too. Some examples?

- "Imagine if I didn't have to ever work weekends again."

- "Imagine if I could afford to send my daughter to private school."

- "Imagine if my friends wanted the same life improvements that I do."

- "Imagine if I wasn't scared of rejection. What would I do then?"

Our minds are powerful, and we can direct our minds to do incredible things.

Are these the only words that work? No.

My good friend, Lloyd Daley, uses these words: "Let's pretend."

When his new team members do not want to set goals, he realizes their brains prevent them from positive expectations. He bypasses those brain programs by telling his new team members, "Let's pretend."

Some examples.

- "Let's pretend that you were successful in our business. How would you feel then?"

- "Let's pretend you received an extra $500 every month. What would you spend it on?"

- "Let's pretend you did earn a car with our company. What would you do with your old car?"

- "Let's pretend you earned enough in our business that you didn't have to go to your job anymore. How would your family feel about that?"

- "Let's pretend you replaced your full-time income with our business. What would be your new plan for life?"

These few words can tell our brains to stop thinking of the negative present, and dream about a positive future. Let's help our prospects visualize a better future.

PLACING NEW INFORMATION INTO OUR PROSPECTS' BRAINS.

If we talk, and no one believes us, are we wasting our efforts? Yes.

It is not only our words that count. What else is important? Our prospects' brains need to accept and believe our words. Acceptance and belief are not automatic. We have to put forth an effort to make this happen.

We can't assume our prospects will smile and say, "I am not skeptical at all. I will believe everything that you say." Well, it could happen, but I haven't seen it happen yet.

As network marketers, we believe in our company and our opportunity. We have a message to tell our prospects. Unless our prospects believe our message, we're wasting our time.

Thankfully, placing a simple bit of information inside our prospects' brains is easy to do. We will learn to format our information in a way that doesn't trigger brain skepticism and salesman alarms. The format is:

Fact, fact, small bit of information.

This is a basic format that puts brain filters to sleep so that new information can enter the brain.

Network marketing pro Jim Stevens posted this on social media. This is a great explanation and example of this easy-to-use technique.

• • •

Think about our products, services, and offerings. We will be able to come up with two facts that pertain to them. And then we'll follow those facts with a small bit of information about what we offer.

It will slide right into their brains, unquestioned, because we just told them two things their brains know to be absolutely true. So the brains say, "Welcome, new information!"

Example:

Fact #1: "A lot of people have gained some new stay-at-home pounds and inches." (No argument if our prospect is clearly carrying some of those pounds.)

Fact #2: "And if they do manage to trim them off ... the next mission is keeping them off." (Again, no issues with arguing the obvious. They are still wearing their extra pounds.)

Small bit of information: "But some people have found a pretty cool drink that pulls off those pounds and inches, and they're able to keep them gone now."

What are our prospects going to say? "Oh well, you can forget me! I am proud of these 15 pounds and two new inches around my belly." Of course they won't say this.

But what happened? Our prospects now believe there is a drink that will take off these pounds, and will probably ask us for details.

• • •

This "fact, fact, small bit of information" formula is from a previous Big Al book. Jim uses this formula to get great results.

Why does this work?

If our brains are in a good mood, and the new information seems reasonable, we accept that new information as true. No questions asked.

How do we put brains into a good mood? By telling our prospects' brains facts that they believe are true. We start off with agreement.

After fact #1, our prospects' brains say, "Yes. That is entirely true."

After fact #2, our prospects' brains say, "That is true also. You must be a genius just like me."

At this point our prospects' brains think, "This is a credible source of new information. I can trust whatever this source says from now on. I have other things to do with my limited brainpower."

Then, we introduce a new piece of information that is readily accepted by our prospects' brains. As long as this new information seems reasonable, we'll have no problems.

Ready for some examples?

- "No raises this year. We are lucky the company is still in business. We should do something now, because the situation won't get better."

- "We don't get paid enough. And then the government takes money out of our paycheck for taxes. This plan is not working."

- "Growing old hurts. And every afternoon is a drag. But some people have figured out a way to have energy all day long."

- "Wrinkles give us character. But I don't need any more of them. We should do something to stop the wrinkling now."

- "Everyone gets utility bills. Most people get overcharged. We can build a good business by helping them reduce their energy bills."

- "Begging our boss for a raise is embarrassing. We even have to ask permission for a day off. We are grown adults now. Maybe we should be our own bosses."

Do we feel how safe and non-threatening these sentences are? Want to get a small bit of information into our prospects' brains, so our prospects can make better decisions? This is an easy technique to master and use.

"DOES OUR BOSS MURDER BABY RABBITS AT HOME?"

We say to our coworker, "I wonder if our boss murders baby rabbits at home."

What happens? Our coworker now associates our boss with the murders of baby rabbits. Now, we didn't say our boss actually did this dastardly deed. But the memory association is there. It will be hard for our coworker to think of the boss without mentally picturing baby rabbit genocide.

This is how our brain stores memories—by association. We connect new memories to something we already know.

Every word we say will have memory associations for our prospects. This is obvious. If you're skeptical, try this experiment.

Start a presentation by saying, "Now, this is not an illegal pyramid."

Will this opening sentence bring up bad associations in our prospects' minds? Yes. At this point we can save time, give up, and return home.

This little experiment should prove to us that we must be careful with our word choices. Ready for another experiment? Look for the troublesome word in this sentence.

"I want to give you a presentation."

Obvious, isn't it? When we say the word "presentation," what associations will come to our prospects' minds?

- Throwing away money.

- Salesman in suits.

- Boring.

- Never ends on time.

- Sleazy promises.

- That three hour in-home meeting I hated.

- Endless PowerPoint slides.

- Scary used-car salesman.

Hmmm. Now we think, "We shouldn't use the word "presentation" when asking for an appointment. It seems to build resistance from our prospects." Yes, this seems obvious. Until we fix this problem, our results will suffer.

What word could we use instead? We need a word that brings up fewer negative associations in our prospects' minds.

Let's try this word: "Options."

What comes to mind when we hear "options?"

- I get to choose.

- No salesman pressure.

- The GPS option on my car.

- Bresler's 33 flavors of ice cream.

- I pick what is right for me.

- People should have choices.

- I love options, especially at buffets.

By substituting "options" for the word "presentations," we create better memory associations in our prospects' minds.

Now, everyone has different word associations. For example, the word "work" can have different associations from individual to individual. Some associations might be security, self-worth, showing love of family, and accomplishment. For others, the associations might be mind-numbing boredom, disgusting waste of time, and being treated as a pawn with no rights.

We should be careful about the words we use that might trigger negative associations.

Can we plant positive word associations by choosing better words?

Yes.

An amateur invitation to an opportunity meeting: "Please come to our opportunity meeting on Tuesday night. Our presentation will tell you all about our business."

A professional invitation to an opportunity meeting: "On Tuesday night, let's look at one more option that could work. There will be pizza at this get-together."

Associations flood our prospects' minds. "Pizza? Thick or thin crust? I love cheese. Cheese makes everything taste better. The best time of my life was when we went to Rome and ate at a local pizzeria. I can still smell it now."

Which invitation will get better results? The answer is obvious.

At this point, we think, "I should review every word I say to check for possible negative associations." Good idea. We could sabotage our efforts with a poorly-chosen word.

Here are some possible word and phrase substitutes. Please remember that everyone is different, so let's use common sense.

- "Calling family and friends for appointments" versus "Giving family and friends a chance for something better."
- "Drink this protein shake every morning" versus "Enjoy a delicious protein shake for breakfast."
- "Save money on your holiday travel" versus "Create lifelong family travel memories for less."
- "Distributor" versus "Connector."
- "Distributor agreement" versus "Adoption form." (I will adopt and mentor you.)

How we say things makes a difference.

HOW TO OVERCOME AN AMBITION DEFICIT.

Do you experience motivation issues?

Do you feel discouraged because a task looks too large?

Do you feel too tired to work, but not tired enough to sleep?

What is the default response to this? "Be miserable, and do nothing."

This is not the success recipe we dream about. It's time for us to take control of our brains.

Something is better than nothing.

Imagine our project requires eight hours of focused work. In our present mental state, that is seven hours and 59 minutes too much. Our strategy?

Step #1: Give up our utopian dream of eight hours of focused work. Release the feelings of guilt.

Step #2: Tell our brains we will only do a few minutes and then take the rest of the day off. This creates a small surge of energy in us.

Step #3: Get into action immediately with a small, easy step.

The result? The worst-case scenario is that we get a few minutes of focused work accomplished. That is a small win for us.

We overcome our unmotivated feelings. We stop our current work paralysis. We start taking action.

Before, we had eight hours of work staring us in the face. Now we start with at least a few minutes of progress. Our net gain is a few minutes of work.

"But I can't even kickstart my first few minutes!"

Idea #1: Start with a five-minute break. Taking a break before we start feels good. We've only committed to a few minutes anyway. This sounds better than starting eight hours of focused work.

Idea #2: Take a 30-second baby step. Once we start our project, we break our mind's resistance. Now we are starting with a little momentum.

Idea #3: Stop using brute force on our minds. Stop chanting, "I will do this!" Instead, give our minds a chance to activate ambition by asking, "Can I do a few minutes?" This gives our minds a chance to pick up the challenge and then say, "I will do this!"

Idea #4: Coffee! Imagine prospecting is our nightmare project, waiting for us to get into action. We hate prospecting. Our results stink! We have a bad attitude.

Enter coffee. We love coffee. We tell our brains, "I will only prospect over coffee. I will meet prospects and give my prospects another option for their lives while I enjoy my coffee."

But what if our prospecting skills get poor results? Then we have to meet even more prospects over coffee. Yes, more coffee! We win even more ... coffee!

We could tell our brains, "I am only 120 coffees away from success."

HOW TO TAKE A RISK.

Successful people know how to manage risk. If they didn't, they wouldn't be successful.

Committing to an activity requires risk. The risk could be our time, or our money. We want to avoid excessive risk.

If we take a risk, we expect a good return on our time and money investments. There is no need to take a risk if our reward will only be one dollar.

Our brains worry and fear the unknown. When this happens, we procrastinate. The problem? If we make no decisions in life, we can't move forward. Here is a basic three-step formula that successful people use.

Step #1: Make sure the best outcome is something we want.

Step #2: Decide if this outcome is worth taking a risk.

Step #3: Identify the worst possible outcome. Can we live with this outcome?

This is pretty simple. Let's apply this formula to a prospect looking to join our business opportunity.

Step #1: Make sure the best outcome is something we want.

The prospect thinks, "Yes, I definitely want a second income and a chance to be my own boss. This would be a dream come true for me."

Step #2: Decide if this outcome is worth taking a risk.

The prospect thinks, "The reward is huge for me. Yes, I am willing to take a risk and invest $300 and some weekend time to make it happen."

Step #3: Identify the worst possible outcome. Can we live with this outcome?

The prospect thinks, "The worst possible outcome for me would be to get zero results. I would lose $300 and miss a few weekends. That's not the end of the world. I could still move on with my life."

Now, our prospects may not have this exact formula clear in their minds, but this is how they think. If our prospects hesitate or procrastinate, following this formula will help move the process to a decision.

THE BEST WAY TO LEARN OR SOLVE A PROBLEM?

Charlie Munger is an investing genius. For decades, he has used common-sense approaches to learning and solving difficult problems. And he is funny too.

His advice?

Think of the inverse. Turn the problem upside down. Attempt to have the opposite thinking as our goal.

For example, imagine we wanted to lose weight. We would ask ourselves, "What could I do to gain more weight?"

And then avoid the answers to this question. That could give us new perspectives for our diet.

If we look at challenges and problems from a different viewpoint, we can gain new insights.

We do this by asking this question:

"What would I do to make this problem worse?" (Then avoid doing that.)

Ready for example questions for our business?

- What could I do to push prospects away?
- What could I do to bore my prospects?
- What could I think so I would no longer believe in my company?
- What would I do to prevent personal motivation?

- What words would I use to turn off prospects?
- Which closing methods would make me cringe?

We can use this "opposite" technique to help our team believe their actions can change their careers. If they don't believe their actions make a difference, we could ask them:

"Could you do something in the next 24 hours to make your life worse?"

They will answer, "Of course!"

And now they believe what they do makes a difference for their future.

Our follow-up question?

"Then, could you do something in the next 24 hours to make your business better?"

They have to agree.

"THE FEAR OF LOSS IS GREATER THAN THE DESIRE FOR GAIN."

We do more to avoid pain and loss than we do to get rewards.

Rewards have limitations when we are trying to motivate someone to take action. If the action is difficult, most people give up on the reward and choose to sit at home and watch television instead.

But if there is a painful problem, people will work harder and longer to eliminate the pain.

Imagine we wanted our new team member to study harder to learn closing skills. Our team member complains, "I miss my favorite television shows. This won't pay off before my next credit card payment is due anyway. Why do I have to do this now?"

A weak answer from us: "If you study hard and use kinder and more effective closing techniques, you can start building your residual income." Yawn. Boring. Uninspiring.

A stronger answer from us: "Remember what your relatives told you? They told you that if you started this business, you would fail! You wouldn't succeed. You made a terrible decision. Now, you don't want to go back to your relatives and hear, 'I told you so. See? You will never succeed.'"

Which answer will motivate our team member to study harder? The answer is obvious. We can change our thinking from "learning more stuff" to "proving our relatives wrong!" We don't want to lose our reputation and damage our self-esteem.

Let's do another example for our unmotivated team member who doesn't want to learn new skills. Again we will use the motivation of proving others wrong.

A weak answer from us: "Studying hard now will pay off in the future when you meet prospects. This is your time to prepare so you will know what to say." True, but uninspiring.

A stronger answer from us: "Remember when you told me your high school classmates voted you 'least likely to succeed?' That hurt. That pain won't go away until you prove them wrong. Here is your chance. You have control over your future business. You don't have to wait for some boss to give you a tiny raise. Let's learn the basic closing skills now so we can create the success you wanted. Let's prove them wrong."

Fear of loss. Fear of embarrassment. Fear of being left behind. For motivating people to take action, fear is better than rewards.

YOU ARE A WORKAHOLIC! NO LIFE BALANCE.

We hate our work. We feel terrible waking up early to go to our mind-numbing job. We look forward to weekends. We dream of our annual holiday. We spend most of our waking hours in misery, hating our job.

This doesn't sound very appealing, does it?

Yet, many people default to this way of life. They rationalize their circumstances by saying they have to make a living. They have to work somewhere. This is their fate in life.

But does life have to be this way? Could we change how our brain thinks about our work? And what if our work was so enjoyable, we didn't need time off from our daily work?

Sound impossible?

The tale of two fishermen.

John's life as a fisherman is hard. Waking up early in the cold mornings, he joins the boat crew for a hard day at sea. The nets are heavy and the work is non-stop. Any spare time goes to mending and improving the nets. The days are long and brutal. He hates every minute of his work, and refuses to eat fish.

Jerry hates his office job. He spends eight hours at work every day wishing he was fishing. He can fish at the local lakes, the rivers, or the ocean. Fishing is the highlight of his weekends. His annual holiday is three weeks of camping in the woods while fishing every waking moment.

So, is fishing the problem or the solution?

It depends on how we train our minds.

The ideal work and career? Something we do for fun. Then, every day feels like a holiday! Mentally, we would never go to work again. We would have no desire to take time off. That is a happy life.

There are two things we can do to create this life.

1. Try to pick work that we love to do.

2. Mentally decide that we enjoy the work we do.

Will our life be perfect if we do these two things? No. But it will be better and happier.

So how do we feel about our network marketing career? Is it fun? Challenging? Something we enjoy? Here is a quick test.

Saturday morning arrives, the beginning of our weekend off from our job. We could watch early morning cartoons, or we could check our network marketing group volume on our computer. If we voluntarily check our business progress first, that is a good sign that we enjoy our business.

But what about those activities we don't enjoy in our network marketing business? Can we change how we think about them? Can we make those activities feel more enjoyable? Yes. Here is an example.

A shy, introverted green personality may hate doing follow-up calls. But, maybe the green personality could change his viewpoint and consider these calls as statistical research. Yeah, accountants and engineers think this way. The calls now feel easier to make.

We can direct our human brains to view unpleasant tasks differently. The solution isn't perfect, but it will make us feel better.

Ultimately, we want to have a career that we love so much, we don't feel like we have to take a holiday away from it. This makes our days happier.

A great example of making our career fun is Jonathan Yap. As a green personality, he won't be cold-calling strangers for appointments. Instead, he will meet anyone and everyone over coffee, a meal, or dessert. Why? Because food is the national sport of Singapore, where he lives.

Take a moment and think about what we love to do. Then ask ourselves, "Can we incorporate our passion into our careers?"

CASH IS REAL. "NOW" IS REAL.

We order our favorite coffee from the local overpriced coffee shop. We pay extra for the "brand" and the experience.

But today, the credit card machine breaks. We have to pay cash. When we reach into our pocket and pull out our limited cash, we think, "This coffee is expensive."

Paying cash creates immediate pain. Our money is gone.

Paying by credit card doesn't feel so bad. This makes it easier to add an overpriced donut to our overpriced coffee order.

When we make our offers to our customers, if we have credit card availability, let them know. This makes their decision easier as they don't suffer the pain of losing their cash.

"Now" is real.

Here is our choice:

1. Do I want immediate pain?

2. Do I want the pain delayed to a later date in the future?

Humans default to choice #2. We will let our future selves deal with the pain then.

This is what happens when we set New Year's goals. It is Friday night, December 31. We tell ourselves, "I need to set my goals for next year. Every morning I will wake up and go to the gym. And I will stop eating sugar."

This is easy to say on December 31. We don't need to do anything right now. We can go back to drinking beer and champagne. Let our January 1 self worry about the self-discipline problem.

How can we use this concept in our network marketing business? These are some examples of conversations with our prospects.

> Us: "It is $700 to join. This pays for starting inventory and training."
>
> Prospect: "No."
>
> Us: "You can use a credit card. You won't have to pay for 30 days. By then, you will have sold a lot of your inventory."
>
> Prospect: "Okay. Makes sense."

"Pay now, or pay later." This is an easy decision for our prospects to make.

Another example?

> Us: "Can we set an appointment for tomorrow evening?"
>
> Prospect: "No."
>
> Us: "How about on Monday, three weeks from now?"
>
> Prospect: "Okay. I will put it on my calendar."

It is true. The further into the future we ask for an appointment, the more our success rate goes up.

The Disney World experience.

Our family needs a vacation. Why not Disney World? We are on a budget, so we will pay cash as we go.

Why are we paying cash? We don't want to increase our credit card debt. We currently have high monthly minimum payments, and we've learned our lesson. Cash is king.

We cringe every time we pay for gas on our trip to Disney World. We see our pocketful of cash getting smaller every time we refuel. Meals along the way seem more expensive when we pay cash. Finally we arrive and prepay our hotel with cash. Yikes. That immediately makes our cash roll smaller.

Disney World admission tickets? There is nothing fun about that purchase. Each person in the family needs their own expensive ticket. Ouch! Our roll of cash shrinks even more.

Who knew that meals inside of Disney World were that expensive? Everyone in the family wants to eat. And drinks? Why are they so thirsty?

The children want a few souvenirs. We know we could buy them cheaper elsewhere.

This is painful. Our cash roll shrinks with every activity and experience during our family vacation. Did we have a good time? Maybe. But we would experience less stress by avoiding the constant pain of paying cash for every tiny experience.

This is why all-inclusive holidays feel better. We don't care how much the family needs. We don't care how thirsty they are. We don't care which activities they choose. This is a holiday, and we can enjoy it to the maximum. Yes, the one-time pain of paying for all-inclusive hurts, but the pain does not come back hourly during the holiday.

Now, what was the cost difference between pay-as-you-go versus the all-inclusive vacation?

That depends.

But what was the difference in happiness between pay-as-you-go versus the all-inclusive holiday?

Huge.

What can we learn from this?

Our prospects don't want piecemeal solutions. They want an all-inclusive price that their minds can understand. When we make things complicated with too many options, we create pain for our prospects.

Some examples of making things too complicated?

"This is our normal retail price. This is our preferred customer price. If you register for auto shipment, you would pay this price. Of course, when you order bundles of three or more, you will save an extra 10%." Groan. These types of explanations damage our brains. Stop.

Our prospects don't spend their days thinking about these options. What happens? We push all these options on to our customers and hope they can sort them out in seconds. This is cruel.

"You can join for the membership fee, and get a 15% discount. Or you can get our Bronze package, our Silver package, or our Gold package. You can maximize your bonuses with this automatic program. And I recommend that you enroll in our monthly training series."

Already our prospects feel overwhelmed.

"If you use two of our services, you will qualify for a 2% discount. This discount accumulates for 12 months. At the end of 12 months, if you have paid on time, you will receive a rebate check that reflects a 2% discount. However, if you get three more services you can qualify for our loyalty club. Our loyalty club …"

Okay. We get the picture. Let's not torture our prospects.

Whenever we can, simplify. Let's make a package price. If we can't make a simple package price, how can we reduce the options and make things simple for our prospects?

We think about our business every day. Our prospects don't. They have their own lives. We occupy only a small slice of time in their day. They don't want to invest time thinking about these options. Having too many options will fatigue their brains, and may trigger "this is getting expensive" thinking.

Our two lessons?

1. Delay the pain.

2. Make our offers simple.

HOW TO CHANGE OUR PROSPECTS' MINDS.

Step #1: Prepare visual charts to prove our presentation.

Step #2: Get testimonials to support our position.

Step #3: Research cold, hard facts that no one could question.

Step #4: Present the truth to our prospects.

Who could argue with this sensible approach? No one.

Unfortunately, this approach has a 0% success rate. Our prospects don't change their minds.

Psychologists call this confirmation bias. We have our beliefs. When we see information that supports our beliefs, we take in that information. Now our beliefs become stronger.

But what happens when we see new information that doesn't support our beliefs? We ignore it. We don't believe it. We give it little credence.

Let's see this in action.

Imagine we prefer a certain model of car. We go to YouTube to watch videos of our favorite car. Which videos will we choose? Will we choose videos that are critical and point out the flaws of our favorite car? Or will we choose to watch the videos that confirm our positive bias for this model of car, and show us a positive story?

We know the answer.

Do we watch the news? There are many news shows to choose from. Do we tend to choose the news show that aligns with our beliefs? Yes. We don't choose the news show with a conflicting point of view.

Our programs, beliefs, and thoughts are like cement in our brains. It will take a lot to change them. We don't change our minds without kicking and screaming.

The problem with changing our minds?

#1. We must admit that we were wrong. We made a mistake. When is the last time a human being volunteered to admit that? It is extremely rare. We hate being wrong. So we make up excuses! We didn't have enough information. We are still right, but the world is wrong. Personal humiliation feels awful. Who wants to admit that they are an idiot? Isn't now a good time to change the subject?

#2. It is too much work to change our minds. Our brains conserve energy. Rethinking, researching, and verifying new facts is a lot of work. Should we do all this work? Or should we relax, keep our current beliefs, and watch our favorite television shows? The choice is obvious.

#3. What we believe becomes part of our identity. Our beliefs become who we are. People describe themselves by saying:

- "I am a Red Sox fan."
- "I am a vegan."
- "I am shy."
- "I am fat."

We can make a longer list, but we get the idea. We tell others that our beliefs show who we are. We don't want to change who we are. Consistency feels better.

But is it possible for us to change our beliefs and still be ourselves?

Think back to when we were six years old. We believed in Santa Claus. We changed our beliefs that Santa Claus wasn't real. He didn't climb down chimneys and didn't have a sled pulled by magical reindeer. Our lives continued. Yes, it was a bit embarrassing. But few of us received psychological damage sufficient to bring in a psychiatrist. We can change.

Empathy + reframing = We have a chance.

Here is one way to minimize the pain our prospects must go through to align with new beliefs.

Step #1: Listen to why they have their irrational, wrong belief. (That's just our opinion, of course.) They have this belief for a reason. We need to identify why this belief is important to them.

Step #2: Try some empathy. Try to put ourselves inside of our prospects' minds. What will happen if they change their beliefs? Will they look silly in front of their friends? Will they become an outcast among their peers? We should try to understand the problems they may face.

Step #3: Reframe the discussion. We cannot attack their beliefs directly. That creates resistance. But with a bit of reframing, we could get them to create a new belief that doesn't embarrass them.

Let's look at an example.

For this example, let's assume we believe there are good and bad people on every football team. We shouldn't prejudge strangers based upon the design of their jerseys.

Our prospects' belief: The people who play for a rival football team are morons, thieves, bad drivers, and overall terrible people. Plus, they don't brush their teeth often enough!

Yes, our prospects hate the rival team. Anyone who plays for that team shouldn't be trusted or respected.

Let's put our three steps to work.

Step #1: Listen to why our prospects have this belief.

Our prospects tell us, "Those people cheat when our football teams play. That is why they always win. And my grandparents lost a huge bet when they won the championship 40 years ago. Because of that gambling bet, my grandparents lost their house. And their car. And they could never take us anywhere. It totally ruined my childhood."

Step #2: Empathy. We step into their shoes and see things from their perspective. In their minds, everyone on the opposing team is responsible for ruining their grandparents' lives. Yes, it is 40 years later, and these are different players, but irrational minds don't follow the rules of logic.

Step #3: Reframing. We start with agreement. Without agreement, we can't move forward. So we start by saying, "I totally agree with you. Grandparents are the best. We don't want anything bad to happen to them. They should be respected and cherished."

So far, so good. We move the focus of our discussion to our common beliefs. Finding common ground gives us a place to start. And we continue our conversation:

"You and I love watching football games. And of course, our wonderful and wholesome home team needs an opponent. We have to have an opposing team so there is a game to watch." (Here, we'll get more agreement from our prospects.)

"I wonder if the members of the opposing team feel the same love for their grandparents?"

Done.

By following these three steps, we have a chance to change our prospects' minds.

Is this guaranteed to work? No. But following the steps at least gives us a chance to change our prospects' minds. If we make new beliefs difficult for our prospects, they won't budge from their current beliefs.

Could we make an argument for the opposite viewpoint? Certainly. We would use the same three steps.

Why people may never let go of their beliefs.

Here are some general guidelines about human nature.

#1. People believe that they know more than they actually do. We discover this when we ask people to explain the reasons for their beliefs. We'll hear a few perspectives, a few facts, and they may even make up a rule that they will follow for life. We have egos. We don't call ourselves dumb. And yes, we think we are smarter than almost everyone else.

An example? Someone insists that the earth is flat. It is held up by a giant tripod built by space aliens. As we listen to their explanation of the facts, we realize our photograph of the world from space is useless. They will continue to believe that they know more than scientists or anyone with a different viewpoint.

#2. A personal experience crushes facts and arguments. It takes time for new information to consolidate into memory. If someone had an experience some time ago, their brains have had plenty of time to consolidate this into memories and beliefs. This won't change because of our facts or "theoretical arguments." We should save our breath.

#3. The human brain has plasticity, the ability to learn and change. Most humans don't use this. We are comfortable with the way things are.

#4. People care about themselves, not others. Our survival program tells us to be selfish and concentrate on surviving. It doesn't allocate much time for other people.

Is it an uphill struggle to change beliefs?

Yes.

The default decision for humans is to keep our current beliefs. We ignore conflicting information and facts.

If we want to change our beliefs, and the beliefs of our prospects, it will take patience and time. Don't expect prospects to listen to our conflicting beliefs and say, "Oh my! I was so wrong. Thank you for enlightening me to the correct way of thinking. I can't believe how misguided I was. You are so smart."

I am still waiting to hear this. It may not happen in my lifetime.

Let's look at another way to work with our prospects' minds.

ASK THE RIGHT QUESTIONS.

Our brains have two parts.

- The conscious mind. The "thinking and awareness" part we use when we are awake.

- The unconscious or subconscious mind. The part that controls most of what we do with pre-arranged programs.

We are using our conscious minds right now while reading this. We are thinking how the brain ideas in this book can affect our lives, and how they can influence others.

Now, we know the conscious mind has limits. It can have one thought at a time. So which part of our brains makes the decisions for our lives?

The subconscious mind!

In the last second, we've made over 100,000 decisions to stay alive. We decided to:

- Blink.

- Move this muscle.

- Contract our left heart ventricle.

- Create 35,000 new digestive enzymes.

- Make new T cells for our immune system.

- Kill thousands of cells, and then create replacements.

- Activate the neuron pathways for a memory.

- Pump blood over there.

And the list goes on and on.

These decisions came from the programs in our subconscious mind.

There. We said it. People do almost everything on autopilot. People spend most of their lives reacting with their subconscious minds.

So what does this mean for us?

We may have trouble controlling our subconscious minds. However, we can definitely mess with other people's subconscious minds. Yes, this happens all the time.

Once we realize most decisions are automatic, we have great power. We can help others make better decisions in their lives. How?

For example, when our prospects have an automatic program that holds them back, what can we do? We can look for a different automatic program that will allow them to say "yes" and move forward. We can choose which program our prospects will use.

Watch this.

I have an automatic program: "I hate exercise!"

It doesn't matter how I developed this program in my past. The reality is that this program keeps me from exercising.

Imagine you want me to exercise by going for a walk. You will search for an alternate program in my mind that will allow a walk. Let's observe this in action.

You: "Want to go for a walk?"

My powerful subconscious mind: "No."

You: "Are you sure? It would be healthy."

My powerful subconscious mind: "No."

You: "Want to go for a walk and get some fresh air?"

My powerful subconscious mind: "No."

You: "Please come for a walk."

My powerful subconscious mind: "No."

You: "Want to walk with me to the donut shop?"

My powerful subconscious mind: "Yes."

Ka-ching! Eureka! So that is how it works.

Decisions come automatically from our stored subconscious minds' programs. These programs are hard for outsiders to change in a few minutes.

Instead of trying to change the program holding prospects back, let's look for a different program that will say "yes" and allow our prospects to move forward.

Remember this rule.

"Asking the right question will get better results than trying to change programs."

Want more examples of asking different questions to access different programs?

- Want to go on a diet? No.
- Want to be thinner? Yes.
- Want to buy expensive vitamins? No.
- Want to be healthier more easily? Yes.
- Can I give you a presentation tomorrow? No.

- Can I give you another option tomorrow? Yes.

- Would you look at my opportunity? No.

- Do you hate your job? Yes.

- Want to start a part-time business? No.

- Want to stop commuting to a job? Yes.

- Are you open-minded to new ideas? No.

- Would you like to know how others are doing this? Yes.

- Want to save money on your utilities? No.

- When you go shopping, do you like paying full price, or do you look for bargains and discounts? Bargains and discounts!!!

This is obvious now. We were asking the wrong questions early in our network marketing careers. The solution is simple.

Ask the correct "yes" question first.

Prospects will have instant gut reactions to our questions. Fighting against their natural gut reactions wastes effort. Instead, let's change our questions so that prospects have positive gut reactions.

FAMILIARITY BREEDS POSITIVE FEELINGS.

When we see something new, our subconscious mind's survival program reacts by saying, "Be careful. This is an unknown. Be skeptical. We don't know what will happen next."

This is the "mere-exposure" effect. Wikipedia defines the mere-exposure effect as when people are familiar with something, they begin to create an emotional bond with it, and therefore prefer it.

Think about coming face-to-face with a Great Dane dog for the first time. If we have survived so far in life, it is because we are cautious. We don't know if this Great Dane will be friendly, or will take off our arm for a snack.

Now, we see this same Great Dane for the second time. Our first experience was friendly and safe. We look forward to scratching behind the Great Dane's ears because he loved it so much in our first encounter. No more fear or skepticism.

This is how prospects judge us. In our first encounter, they will be unsure of our intentions. If the first encounter went well, we feel familiar and safe to them in our second encounter. The more encounters we have, the safer we feel to them.

How to increase our odds of success.

It's simple. Become more familiar.

We can attempt to sell our products or opportunity to prospects the first time we meet. If we use good words, have a great offer, and build rapport, we will have consistent success.

But what if we attempt to sell our products or opportunity the second time we meet? Our prospects will have less skepticism and fear, so our odds of success increase.

While waiting for a second meeting may not always be practical, if we have the option, it would give us a better chance for a fair hearing. Yes, just hanging around increases trust levels.

Here is an example.

Prospects might be skeptical about a home-based business on their first exposure. After their first exposure, they start noticing home-based businesses everywhere. When we meet our prospects again, a home-based business doesn't seem so strange. Now they can open their minds and hear more of our story.

OUR FRAMING AND ANCHORING BIASES.

There is an old saying: "It is not what we say, but how we say it."

With a few misplaced words, we can get the opposite result of what we want. Here are some examples.

A man says to his date: "When I look in your eyes, time stands still."

A man says to his date: "Your face would stop a clock."

Both statements describe the same event. But with a few different words, we frame what we say in a positive or negative light. In this case, this could be the difference between a good date and a bad date.

A child says to the parents: "I finished almost all of my homework."

A child says to the parents: "I have some homework left."

Children know how to manipulate their parents' feelings. In the first statement, the child put a positive spin on not finishing the homework. Children intuitively know not to present unfinished homework with the second statement. The second statement prompts the parents to criticize the unfinished task.

Framing tells our prospects how to look at what we offer.

When we "frame" our message a certain way, we can tell our prospects to take a certain point of view.

Does framing or positioning make that much difference? Look at this example.

The 18-year-old son borrows the family car. He stays out way too late, and has an accident that totals the car. This is going to be a difficult phone call to the parents. How should the son frame this phone call?

> Son: "Mom, Dad. Sorry to wake you up at 1 AM. I have some good news and some bad news."
>
> Parents: "Oh no! Tell us the bad news first."
>
> Son: "I had a bad car accident and wrecked the family car. But the good news is that I am alive."
>
> Parents: "Oh, thank goodness you are alive."

The son smiles at his framing skills. He has a bright future.

Framing skills + Anchoring skills.

A way of looking at framing is that our prospects' minds understand things by comparison. How do we learn new concepts? By comparing the new information with what we already know.

Anchoring gives our prospects' brains a starting point for comparisons. Now, we choose the starting point for comparison, not our prospects.

Let's do some network marketing examples.

We say: "You can buy an inexpensive face cream at the discount store for $10. But our luxury cream and skincare system is $200."

When our prospects compare $10 to $200, our products feel expensive. We started the conversation by using a $10 starting point. Our prospects are "anchored" to $10 as the starting point for comparison.

So let's reframe and re-anchor this. We want our prospects to compare our products to a more expensive option.

We say: "Botox costs a lot. An average treatment is $300-$500 and only lasts a few months. But our luxury cream and skincare system is only $200."

Now the price of our skincare system seems more reasonable to our prospects.

Let's try dieting.

We say: "A cheap breakfast at a fast food restaurant is at least $10, and will make us fat. Ten days of our breakfast diet shake only costs $30. You save money, lose weight, and don't have to stand in line."

How about our opportunity? Can we present the opportunity to join our business in a more favorable light, and in a way that makes a decision to join easier for our prospects? Of course.

First, let's look at a bad example.

We say: "At your job, they pay for your training. And you get paid for all the hours you work. But when you start a new business with us, you must take cash from your pocket to pay for your training and your startup costs."

This won't go over well. Let's try again. This time let's anchor the comparison to something more expensive like a traditional business. Then our startup costs will feel reasonable.

We say: "If you are like most people, you want to start your own business to have time freedom and to earn more money. But, you have common sense. You don't want to pay tens of thousands of dollars to start a business and then lose that money if the business fails. That would be devastating. You want a safer solution. You can start our home-based business for less than $500. You won't be risking your family's financial security. And you can do this part-time without jeopardizing your current salary."

This sounds so much better. Now prospects will compare our home-based business to the riskier alternative of investing tens of thousands of dollars, and quitting their jobs.

Using better words will affect prospects' decisions.

I scheduled an operation. The surgeon told me what to expect. See if his choice of words and framing makes a difference.

Surgeon: "You have a 2% chance of dying during this operation."

Even with good math skills, this sounds frightening. Would my attitude suffer from this explanation? Yes!

Now, imagine the surgeon explained it to me this way.

Surgeon: "98% of patients have no problem with this simple procedure."

A much better way to start the conversation. As a patient, I would feel more confident.

We have power. We can choose how our prospects look at our products, services, and business opportunities. This explains why two network marketers can have different results while talking to the same prospects. One network marketer knows how to frame and anchor the prospects' thinking. The other network marketer has no idea that this makes a difference.

I HATE THIS, BUT IT WORKS.

I don't have a good relationship with exercise. Some friends have an addiction to exercise. They have gym memberships and jog in circles for no reason. They lift heavy weights only to put them back down again. It doesn't make sense to me.

Then what sold me on exercise?

My hippocampus. This part of our brain is important for learning new things and storing our memories. The hippocampus area shrinks as we grow older. But when we add a bit of exercise? This area of our brain can increase in size and volume. It doesn't take a rocket scientist to figure out that exercise enhances our brains.

So which exercise should I choose? Walking.

Why? First, it is easy. I know how to walk. This doesn't take more training. And I don't need to find a certified walking coach.

The problem with walking? It is incredibly boring. If we walk around the block, we eventually end up where we started. This doesn't seem like an efficient use of effort.

How did I fix this boring problem? I like to learn new things every day. I turn my one-hour walk into a learning academy.

This left me two choices.

Choice #1: Walk and read.

Choice #2: Walk and listen.

I love reading more than listening to audio. However, I did learn that walking and reading at the same time is hazardous to one's health. I have tripped, fallen off curbs, stepped on snakes, and walked into parked cars.

So, I went with choice #2. Now I listen to scientific audios while I walk. I know some people will want to listen to music. Now, I haven't found a practical use for memorizing music lyrics yet. So for me, my preference is science.

I encourage everyone to learn one new thing a day. If we want to build our careers faster, the new thing will be about our business. When we learn one new thing every day, in just three months, 90 days from now, we can be an expert on almost anything. What could we learn?

- How to meet new people within our comfort zone.
- Stress-free ways to get prospects to make an instant decision.
- How to create word pictures inside our prospects' minds.
- The techniques for creating instant rapport.
- How to find new and better prospects for our business.
- The first steps to becoming a leader.
- How to get past our prospects' brain resistance.
- What will make our prospects want to connect with us.
- How to sell without being sleazy.
- How to triple our income by changing what we say and do.

This list can go on and on. But instead of blaming our prospects for our lack of success, we can take the time to learn the skills. And this learning time can double as our exercise time.

Does it make us feel good when we expand the size and volume of our hippocampus area? Yes. And the new skills we learn are a bonus.

One more tip: Write down our most pressing problem before our walk. Then our brain will work in the background to solve this problem during our exercise time.

HOW TO TRICK OUR BRAINS INTO FEELING GOOD.

Feeling down?

Smile.

We'll feel a little better.

Our body sends signals to our brains. If our body language and actions are positive, our brains get that message and decide that we feel better.

Our environment influences our thoughts. If we want our thoughts to improve, an easy step is to improve our environment. That means we can change who we associate with, which types of TV shows we watch, and which actions we take daily.

This is why smiling and exercising will improve our mood. We can use these outside forces to direct our brains into more positive directions.

Here are more things we can do to improve the input to our brains:

- Associate with positive people. This gives our brain extra impressions that life can be good.

- Exercise. Yes, it may be difficult. But exercise causes our brains to release dopamine, norepinephrine, serotonin, and good, positive feelings. We have to find an exercise that we enjoy so that we will do it regularly. Walking, running, dancing, gym workouts, tennis, and running after small children are all good options.

- Dark chocolate. While no one knows the upper limit of dark chocolate that we can eat for this effect, Keith and I will continue to push the limits of this research.

- Meditation. It can be hard to slow down and quiet our minds if we are beginners. Thankfully, the internet has plenty of audios we can download to play in the background. These will help us experience the stress-relieving feelings we get from a short meditation.

- Help the unfortunate. A bit of charity work that helps the less-fortunate will make us feel better and appreciate what we have.

- Singing. This is for us, not for others. And if we sing off-key, sing in private so we won't induce depression and anxiety in others.

- Smile, and our faces will tell our brains to be happier. As a side benefit, others will respond to us more positively. This creates more feedback that affects our brains.

- Laugh. Read something funny. Watch a good comedy movie. And if we fall into a deep, dark depression, maybe some dark satire will be our first step out. When we laugh, good hormones flood our bodies.

- Listen to our favorite upbeat music. With millions of songs to choose from, we can create the perfect playlist that makes us feel good. If we don't know where to start, most people feel a positive attachment to the music from their teens.

- Yoga. (Not yogurt.) Yoga reduces our stress and lowers our cortisol levels. Plus, if we do our yoga with friends, the social environment will make us feel even better. Join a class.

Of course we won't do everything in the list, but we should at least pick one thing that feels comfortable for us. Yes, if that means doubling or tripling our dark chocolate intake, at least we are taking a step in the right direction. And who knows? The extra dark chocolate might make us feel like taking a walk.

What will be our plan? Here is an example.

When I feel down, I will immediately:

- Smile.
- Watch a good comedy for belly laughs.
- Eat a few dark chocolate bars.
- Listen to my favorite upbeat songs.

We can choose how we want to control our brains.

"HAVE TO" VS. "GET TO."

I am not a morning person. My thoughts about waking up early? Well, those thoughts are ugly.

Humans hate paying taxes. I am human. I don't look forward to all that wasted time accumulating the paperwork for my tax returns.

The list of things that I hate go on and on. Everyone has a "most hated" list.

How can we fool our brains into looking at our hated tasks in a more positive way?

We change the words in our thinking.

When we say we "have to" do something, that creates negative feelings. We have no motivation for this task. Plus, we create resistance to the task. The end result? We procrastinate forever. This makes us feel guilty.

When we say we "get to" do something, that creates positive feelings. We appreciate the chance to do this task. Now our procrastination genes can be suppressed.

Let's look at some examples.

Before: "I hate waking up in the morning."

After: "I get to wake up in the morning. This is better than the alternative."

Before: "I hate paying taxes."

After: "I get to pay taxes because I earned more money."

Before: "I hate meeting new prospects."

After: "I get to meet new prospects who may want to join my business."

Before: "I hate closing prospects."

After: "I appreciate the chance to ask them if now is a good time for them or not."

Two words.

This seems so easy. Why? Because it is easy!

We can control how we talk to our minds. We don't have to be victims.

We don't need any training to use these two words. Anyone can start using "get to" immediately.

"UH ... UH ... I FORGOT WHAT YOU SAID."

Our short-term memory is ... short!

How many thoughts can we keep in our short-term memory? Not many. As we add new thoughts, our short-term memories push our old thoughts away, never to be recovered.

Short-term memory is separate from long-term memory. It takes a while for the brain to process and store something in our long-term memory. We don't want to store everything. If we did, our brains would fill up quickly.

Have we ever had someone talk to us too fast with too many facts? What did our brains do? Give up! Too much to process. Too much to remember. We only have so much space in our short-term memories.

So are we a short-term memory to our prospects?

Yes.

It's humbling. Everyone would like to be important in other people's lives. But that's not always the case.

Here is a fun test.

Go to a one-hour opportunity meeting. Drive home. Sit down over a cup of tea and tell our spouse what we remembered from the 60 minutes of information. At the three-minute mark, we are running out of things to say. At the six-minute mark, we stare silently into space. This means over 90% of the meeting's great information faded away from our short-term memory already. We will remember even less tomorrow.

We think we are far more important than we are.

So our concern is, "If our prospects are only going to remember a few points from our message, let's choose which points we want them to remember."

Save the best for last!

How can we get our most important points remembered? Mention these good points at the end of our message. Here is roughly the order of what prospects remember:

1. The last things we say.

2. Something exciting about what we say.

3. How we started our conversation.

4. Everything else.

#3, how we started our conversation, may not be remembered. But we do want to start our conversation in a great way or else we will have no audience. And #4, everything else, is forgotten the moment we said it. It's sad, but true.

The Recency Effect.

We remember the end of a conversation better than the beginning of a conversation.

Let's imagine we try to convince someone that our friend would be a great blind date. We say, "Here are his three best characteristics. He is loyal, doesn't party too much, and has a good job."

Then we say, "And here are his three biggest flaws. He makes mistakes, is unreliable, and drinks too much beer."

The three biggest flaws will be easy to remember. Why? Because they were the last things we said. That was a bad strategy.

Obviously we should reverse the order. We should start with his three biggest flaws. And then later mention his three best characteristics.

Now the three best characteristics become easier to remember. They were the last thing we said.

Let's do a bit of planning.

We present our prospects with a chance to buy or join. What should we say for the two or three sentences before our close? This will influence our prospects.

This is the time to talk about our biggest savings, our products' awesome benefits, or our best testimonials. Now these positives are fresh in our prospects' minds.

Here are a few examples to make this strategy easy to remember.

We eat at a new restaurant. The service is mediocre. The food is nothing special. But at the end of our meal the waiter says, "We have a signature dessert that we are famous for. I will bring one of these for each of you. Don't worry, it is complimentary. It is our way of saying 'thank you' for coming to our restaurant this evening."

Assuming the dessert was quite tasty, what is our most recent memory of our restaurant experience? Free dessert!

Free dessert is always better than a free appetizer or starter. Recency matters.

Now we are off to Disney World. When we arrive, our experience isn't like the brochures. The lines are long. The food is expensive. There is a gift shop tempting the children at the end of every ride. The crowds, the heat … well, it is a very tough day.

Closing time. The family is exhausted. Irritable. Arguing. But then, Cinderella stops our family, poses for 50 pictures, tells a story, and we look at our children. Their eyes are the size of manhole covers, and they're smiling from ear to ear! Tears come to our eyes as we feel our children's emotion. It's magical!

So what do we think of our day at Disney World? It was beyond awesome!

Remember the order of what prospects remember?

- The last things we say. (This scene happened as we were leaving Disney World.)
- Something exciting about what we say. (Cinderella works her magic.)
- How we started our conversation. (The memory of how we started the day fades.)
- Everything else. (The day's disappointing activities disappear from our memories.)

Sometimes it is not what we say, but it is the order of what we say that matters.

Timing is everything. If we plan our conversation correctly, we want the most impressive points at the very end. What good are impressive points if our prospects can't remember them?

Let's do another example.

We love our city's sports team. We attend every game. And now, it is the championship game.

The biased referees penalize our team often. Our team performs at a mediocre level at best. Depressing. To compensate, we drink more beer to drown our disappointment.

But in the final minutes, our team scores three times in spectacular fashion and wins the championship. It's a miracle finish that will be replayed for decades. We go from the depths of depression to the ecstasy of a surprise fairytale ending. We celebrate with more beer!

Now, what will be our memories of this game? Let's compare it to our original list:

- The last things we say. (The miracle ending! Yes, recency rocks.)
- Something exciting about what we say. (The three scores are cemented in our minds. And it is great that they happened at the end of the game.)
- How we started our conversation. (The memory of the opening ceremony fades.)
- Everything else. (The first 98% of the game fades from memory.)

What about our ending when we talk to prospects?

Do we have a "wow" product demonstration? Save it for the end.

Do we have a testimonial of someone who purchased a five-star holiday for the price of a cheap hotel stay, and created family memories forever? Yes, we want this in our prospect's memory.

Do we have a case study of a customer saving huge money? We could allude to this in our opening, but save the amazing details for the end of our presentation.

Do we have a story of how someone returned from an all-expenses-paid company holiday?

Do we have a story of how our income opportunity changed someone's life?

Yes, save the best for last.

What about final decisions?

Humans hate the difficult task of deciding what to do next. They think:

- "What if I make the wrong choice?"
- "Do I have all the facts I need?"
- "What if my circumstances change?"
- "Will others laugh at my decision?"

This is stressful. Decisions are hard work.

Can we help make decisions easier for our prospects? Of course.

Instead of open-ended decisions that require lots of independent thought, humans prefer having multiple choices. This is easier for our brains to process. The most basic choices we can give our prospects are these two options:

Option #1: Our wonderful offer.

Option #2: Keep your life the same. Don't do anything.

Our close might sound something like this:

"So what is going to be easier for you? To continue fighting traffic to and from work five days a week? Or to start your part-time business tonight so maybe next year you can work out of your home?"

Two choices. Clear. No other options. That is what humans like.

But what if our prospects want multiple choices? Will our prospects remember three, four, or even five options? Probably not. So let's make sure our preferred option is at the end of the options list, so it will be remembered.

Here are some examples of how we could arrange this ending to our presentation. Notice how the last option feels the best.

• • •

If you are like most dieters, you have choices:

- Exercise until you hurt.
- Take handfuls of pills and hope they will help.
- Guzzle down chalky shakes until we can't do this anymore.
- Put this weight-loss adhesive patch on your arm twice a day.

Which one of these makes sense for your busy life?

• • •

If you are like most homeowners, you have choices:

- Pay the full retail rate of your utility provider, never getting a break on your rate.
- Wonder why your neighbors are paying less for their utilities.

- Continue to feel frustration at the ever-increasing utilities rates.

- Switch to our lower rate and spend the savings on something good for your family.

Which choice feels better for you?

• • •

The good news? We get to arrange the multiple choices however we want. Yes, we can make sure our option is the last choice and easy to remember.

Let's do one more example.

• • •

If we want to earn more money for the family, we have choices:

- Get a part-time job for the rest of our life to supplement our full-time income.

- Hope our boss makes a math mistake and gives us a 50% raise.

- Win the lottery.

- Start a part-time business, and grow it into a full-time income replacement.

Which choice makes the most sense for you?

• • •

If we don't connect and get our message into our prospects' minds, who is at fault? We are. Our prospects are not responsible for making the extra effort to understand us and our offer.

Fortunately, if we put our best points at the very end of our presentations, our prospects will remember.

PUTTING OUR RETICULAR ACTIVATING SYSTEM TO WORK.

"Oh look! Check out that armadillo eating nachos!"

"No, wait! This is more important."

"Did you hear that???"

The conscious, thinking part of our brain is tiny. We can only have one thought at a time.

Underneath our conscious mind, we have a huge ocean of brain activity. This is the subconscious mind, and this part of our mind can serve us well.

The reticular activating system is a function of our subconscious mind that controls what we pay attention to in our environment. It helps us tune out all of the extra noise that is happening around us, so our conscious mind doesn't get overwhelmed with information.

Let's go for a walk.

Millions of bits of information overwhelm our minds every second. Everything we see, the textures, the colors, and the movements flood through our vision. What about sound? What did those sounds mean to us? Should we pay attention to them? Do some of those sounds form a word? Will this word be important to us? What about the different smells?

We get the idea. There is too much information and we can only have one conscious thought at a time. This isn't going to work.

So our subconscious mind has a program that filters out most of this information. We don't have to think about it, store it, process it, or worry about it. If it is the same path that we walk every day, we would only notice something that's dramatically different.

Here is an example. Every day we commute to work amongst other cars. But yesterday, we bought a shiny, bright red car. We love our new car. And guess what? Now we notice the other red cars on the road.

Here's another example. At the airport, we don't pay attention to all the announcements on the loudspeakers. But if they announce our name on the loudspeakers, we instantly notice. Our brain sorts out all the unimportant announcements, and alerts us when we hear our name.

One more example. We walk through a large office building. We don't notice much of our surroundings. Later, after 5 cups of coffee, we panic! "Where are the restrooms?" We didn't notice the restroom signs earlier in the day. Those signs were not important to us at that time. But once we have an urgent need to find the restrooms, we will notice every restroom sign we see.

This explains one of the reasons that goal-setting works. When we have a goal, our subconscious mind will notice resources that can help us reach our goal. If we want to make a pizza tonight, we will notice when we walk by the cheese, the vegetables, and the pepperoni in the grocery store.

If our goal is to locate prospects who hate their jobs, guess what we will notice every day? Yes, we will see job dissatisfaction everywhere.

Most people go through life on autopilot. If we don't have goals, it is easy to miss important resources for our future.

This part of our brain works automatically in the background. We don't have to do much consciously. All we have to do is give this part of the brain a problem or goal, and it will notice resources that can help us.

A simple way to take advantage of this automatic help is to write down our goals and place this list somewhere where we will see it daily. Nothing wrong with reminding our subconscious of what we are looking for.

Another way to use this to our advantage? Give our subconscious a problem to solve while we sleep. We can have sweet dreams while our subconscious silently thinks of new and innovative solutions to our problem. How long does this take? A few seconds before we go to sleep every night.

What to avoid.

Avoid negative thoughts and affirmations. We don't want to train this part of our brains to find reinforcing negatives about ourselves. That is reverse self-improvement, going the wrong way.

Let's not say to ourselves:

- "I am not lucky."
- "These things never work out for me."
- "I am fat."
- "I am too shy to approach people."
- "No one will believe me."
- "I am so disorganized."
- "What else can go wrong today?"

We get the idea. We want to train our minds to find positive evidence to support our growth mindset. We don't want to look for negative evidence that makes us feel bad.

A great analogy is to compare our attention with an apple seed. If we plant an apple seed, we expect an apple tree. If we plant a cherry seed, we expect a cherry tree.

If we plant a certain affirmation or belief in our minds, our subconscious minds will work overtime to find proof to support our beliefs.

We can train our minds to think and notice certain things, so here is one more tip.

Train our minds with positive thoughts. Our minds will then look for proof to support our positive beliefs.

We don't want to say to ourselves, "I am not an ax murderer." Yikes! That brings up some scary imagery.

Instead, we could say to ourselves, "I am a kind, giving person." Now our minds will look for proof and situations where we can practice our kindness for the good of others.

Let's put our subconscious minds to work. It's free labor.

HOW CAN WE MAKE OTHERS PAY ATTENTION TO US?

We talk, but no one is home. It happens to all of us.

We want an engaged audience when we speak.

Here are some quick ways to rivet our prospects' attention.

#1. Ask a question. Now prospects have to pay attention. They have to think about our question so they can answer. What are some fun questions we can ask?

- What do you think is the best way to stay young?
- If you had an extra $500 a month, what is the first thing you would do with it?
- What are the chances you will get a $500 raise from your boss in the next month?
- If you only had to work a four-day week, what would change for you?
- If you could have a dream vacation for the price of a regular vacation, where would you go?
- So what would you do next?
- Do you have another plan to earn more money monthly?
- Do you wonder why things didn't work?

#2. Tell a story. Everyone wants to hear how the story ends. Make sure our story is short and to the point. We can lose our prospects by talking too long and being boring. If we are not natural storytellers, we can use these prompts to begin our story:

- Before I show you how this works, let me tell you what happened to me.
- Imagine this situation.
- This just happened.
- When I was young, my mother told me …
- Does this sound familiar?
- If this happened, what would you do?

#3. Move. Don't be stationary. What movements can we use to draw attention?

- Hand gestures.
- Roll our eyes.
- Change where we are standing or sitting.
- Move in an unpredictable way.
- Start drawing an image so our prospects wonder what it will be.
- Open a package.
- Show something strange.

#4. Get our prospects to do something. Some examples:

- Hold a pen.
- Be part of an experiment.
- Guess a number.
- Write down their best guess.

#5. Humor. This always gets people's attention. However, we should be careful for obvious reasons. We don't want to take someone out of their comfort zone or be offensive.

Imagine going to a stand-up comedy show. Our minds start to drift. Suddenly, the entire audience is laughing. We wonder what we missed. And now our attention is back on the comedian.

What is the safest humor? Self-deprecating humor. If we make fun of ourselves, there is little chance of our prospects getting offended.

#6. Curiosity. Get people interested in what you're going to say next. Some examples?

- Scientists have figured out why our skin wrinkles, and it is not what we thought.

- I always wondered what kind of food took away my energy.

- Of all the things they taught us in school, they got this one wrong.

- What is the one thing we can do before lunch that would most affect our bank account?

- What is the best way to get money to work for us?

- Can you guess the one food that actually burns our body fat while we sleep?

- Do you know the real reason wrinkles start?

- Do you know the first thing that happens when we become our own boss?

There's no room for entitlement here. We can't assume prospects will listen to us.

Prospects don't have an obligation to listen to us. We have to earn the right to their time and attention. But earning the right for their attention is easy with these skills.

STUPID RULES.

Stupid rules hold us back, kill our motivation, and create stress. But here's the thing.

We created these stupid rules!

How do we do this to ourselves?

Have we ever said any of these things to ourselves?

- "I will be happy when ..."
- "I will be happy if ..."
- "I must achieve this goal by ..."
- "If they don't reply, I will feel ..."
- "If they say 'no,' I will feel ..."

Sound familiar?

When we create these artificial rules, restrictions, and measurements, we set ourselves up for dissatisfaction. This is a good time to reduce our requirements for happiness and success.

We may be thinking, "Don't we need goals and progress reports to be successful? Don't we have to measure?" No.

And then we remember this saying: "It can only be improved if it can be measured."

But that's not correct.

We don't need measurement and external pressure to move our business forward.

Before we prejudge this alternate concept, let's dig in a little.

THE HIDDEN FLAW IN GOALS.

Are goals the best way to measure our lives? Maybe not.

There are two downsides with goals:

1. We don't reach our goal and feel bad.

2. We reach our goal and feel bad.

This is a lose-lose situation. We set up our minds for disappointment.

First, let's look at what happens when we set goals and don't achieve them. Our unfulfilled goal is a constant reminder of our inadequacy. Our reaction? Guilty feelings for not working harder to achieve our goals. A feeling of deficiency looms darkly in our brains. If we do this often enough, this could become an affirmation: "I am a loser."

Second, let's look at what often happens when we set goals and achieve them. After a brief moment of celebration, then what? Empty emotions. We think, "I thought I would enjoy this moment more."

We missed appreciating the journey experience. Yes, much of the joy is in the journey, not the final destination.

If this is how our minds think, a simple change will increase our happiness.

Let's focus on the journey, the feelings, and the activities that we do instead of the final goal.

Imagine we decide to lose weight by exercising at the local gym daily. We could dread our daily visits to the gym. We look forward to our brief moment of happiness when we reach our ideal weight.

Instead, could we find a way to enjoy our daily visits to the gym? That would put a bit more happiness in our days. When we enjoy the process, not only will we continue the process, but it is fun.

But ... what can we use in place of goals?

Let's see.

HABITS AND SYSTEMS.

We have habits for so many little things in our day. No thinking involved. Imagine brushing our teeth in the morning. Washing our hands before meals. Putting our socks on before our shoes. We don't waste brainpower making these decisions.

Earlier in our lives, we turned these activities into habits. No more willpower needed.

We have good habits and bad habits. Both are easy and automatic.

And systems? Systems focus on an activity that will give us predictable results. An example of a system?

Controlling our weight. These could be steps in our system:

- Only buy healthy foods at the store.
- Make sure to have low-calorie snacks available at all times.
- Find a walking partner.
- Eat a healthy miniature meal before going out to eat with friends.
- Become allergic to ice cream. (Okay, that's a bit too far.)

When we follow the rules of our system, we know the outcome will be in our favor. We can enjoy our system every day without the stress of restrictive goals and constant measuring.

Should we never set goals? Should we never set up progress checkpoints?

That is a personal decision. We all have different wiring in our brains.

What is an example of a system to build our business?

Let's first think of the activities that get results. Here are a few of them:

- Send 5 "thank you" messages every morning. People love appreciation.
- Ask every new person we meet, "What are you working on now?"
- Learn one new idea a day that can help our business.
- Tweak and improve how we explain our business in a sentence or two.
- Look for new places and opportunities to comfortably meet new friends.

Are these ways not for us? Maybe try some other ways:

- Make one phone call to a prospect who could be a potential leader.
- Follow up with a prospect and ask for a recommendation.
- Read a chapter of a book on sales and learn how we can get our message across more effectively.
- Call a satisfied customer and ask how we can help more.
- Say "hi" to one more person today.
- Take the time to make a reply more personal.
- **Smile** to three more people today.

We get the idea. We can customize our system to fit our personalities and comfort zones.

Some people want an aggressive "build it fast" list of activities. Others? They want to have the business fit in with the other parts of their lives.

Do we all have to build in the exact same way? No.

We get to choose.

So why not design our system in a way that makes us happy?

"FAKE IT UNTIL YOU MAKE IT!" REALLY???

I am standing outside of my prospects' door. This couple has influence. They are successful. If I can convince them to join my business, this would be my first step to moving up in the ranks.

Am I nervous? Yes. So far no one has joined. Everyone took one look at me, and then decided, "No." I didn't even need a presentation to get rejected. I could get rejection immediately. It turns out I was an expert at getting instant rejection.

Before I pressed the doorbell, I went through my mental checklist.

- Smile.
- Tell ourselves we are great.
- Imagine a successful outcome.
- Chant, "I make my dreams come true."
- Affirm, "I am successful already."
- Dress for success.
- Speak in a lower, confident voice.
- Full eye contact, just short of glaring.
- Become one with the universe.
- Feel the burn.

Yeah! I was so ready.

Apparently my prospects were not so ready. They refused to answer the door, pretending that no one was home.

No problem. I believed in the power of persistence. I kept ringing. I had no quit in me!

Finally my prospects answered their door.

One quick look at my face and they said, "I am sorry. We talked about this. We decided we are not interested."

Done. Failure. All it took was a simple look at my face.

What did they see?

Many decisions and judgments happen before we say our first word.

My prospects read my micro-facial expressions. They saw my body language. They saw my eyes. They observed a nervous young man pretending to be brave. Prospects know.

There is an old saying: "What we believe is so loud that people can hear it."

What is a better plan?

Instead of pretending, I should have worked on becoming what I wanted to project.

"Fake it until we make it?" There is a certain odor this creates that doesn't pass our prospects' "smell test" when they first meet us.

Another way of looking at this old saying? "Fake it until we come to our senses."

Then, as soon as possible, build our belief in what we offer. If we are authentic, prospects know.

LEARN FAST. TEACH FAST.

The fastest way to learn new things?

By comparing new information with something we know. That is why stories, analogies, examples, and metaphors work so well. Our brains struggle with new, abstract, and unfamiliar concepts or ideas.

Imagine we look at a picture of a bottle with a plain background. Is the bottle large? Small? We don't know. We have nothing to compare it with. It will take a lot of work and investigation to guesstimate the bottle's dimensions.

Now, let's redo that picture. Again the picture is of a bottle with a plain background, but we place a hand in the picture. Now our brain compares the bottle's size to a human hand. We learn the size of the bottle in less than one second. That is the power of comparing new information to what we already know.

What is the amygdala, and why is it important?

"The amygdala is one of two almond-shaped clusters of nuclei located deep and medially within the temporal lobes of the brain's cerebrum in complex vertebrates, including humans." Wikipedia is so helpful. Now we can forget that definition without too much trouble. Yes, this description will be meaningless to most.

Cognitive psychologists and neuroscientists love using these accurate, useless phrases. We hear this new information, but because these words don't relate to anything we currently know, we don't even attempt to remember it.

Now, let's compare this to something we already know. How is this for a definition that would feel useful to us?

"The amygdala is the emotional part of our brain that makes us happy, mad, afraid, and appreciative of rewards."

Ah, now that makes more sense. We understand this part of the brain deals with our emotions. All we need is a simple comparison, and in an instant, we understand.

A secret of fast learning is to attach or compare the new information to something we know. With this secret, we will learn and more importantly, remember more quickly.

Can we use this secret to communicate our message to our prospects? Yes!

Think of all the things we understand in our business that our prospects don't. We've already attended training. Our prospects haven't. Total group volume, line of sponsorship, rank promotion? These terms have no meaning to our prospects. It is our job to use stories, analogies, examples, and metaphors to communicate these concepts to prospects.

A quick way to remind ourselves to explain better? Use the words, "Which means."

Let's use an example of "which means" in our explanation.

Prospects: "How does group volume affect our bonus check?"

Us. "We get paid on group volume, which means that the more people who use our products, the bigger our paychecks. If we have fewer people using our products, we earn less."

Notice how we avoided math in our answer. Math tends to be abstract and hard to visualize.

Another example.

Prospects: "Why is your patented extract concentration important?"

Us: "Extract concentration puts more power in our capsules, which means we only have to take one capsule a day instead of handfuls of pills. Customers love this."

Try to use "which means" often. Not only is it effective, but it is also polite.

But what about stories, analogies, examples, and metaphors? Let's do some now.

A story to help prospects feel comfortable talking to their relatives and friends.

"When I got started, I was shy and embarrassed about talking to my brothers and sisters about my new business. Instead of talking to them, I talked to acquaintances and strangers. Well, news of my new part-time business got back to my brothers and sisters. They called me and asked, 'Why didn't you talk to us first? At least you could give us an option to say yes or no. We thought you cared about us.' Not only was I embarrassed, I felt bad about not sharing with the people I loved."

Prospects can feel our discomfort in telling this story. They too have relatives and close friends. Now they understand why they should talk to them first.

Next, an analogy that explains residual income.

> "Our customers will use our service every month. Even though we only talked to them one time, we get paid a residual income month after month when they pay their monthly bill. It is like writing a hit song one time, and getting royalties month after month. We do something right one time and get paid over and over again."

This is easy for our prospects to understand. Now the term "residual income" has meaning in their minds.

Use an example? Easy to do.

> "How do we market and sell this product? Easy. People either want it, or not. All we do is give them an option, stand back, and let them decide. Here is an example. The waitress asks us, 'Do you want cream in your coffee?' Then she stands back and lets us decide. That is exactly what we do for people."

If our prospects were holding back from joining our business because they were imagining themselves giving high-pressure sales presentations, this little example solves their misunderstanding. Easy.

Use a metaphor for better understanding? Sure. Let's do one now.

"These diet capsules fire up the fat-burning furnaces in our bodies, and fuels them 24 hours a day." This metaphor is easier to picture than explaining the metabolic facts.

If we didn't use this fat-burning metaphor, our explanation would sound like this: "Our brain signals the fat cells to release fatty acid molecules into our bloodstream. Then our body picks up these fatty acids and uses their energy."

Not very useful to the amateur dieter listening to our diet sales presentation.

Our goal is to learn fast and teach fast. Using these tools can help.

SUMMARY.

Now we have many brain rules and mindset ideas that we can put to use. It is up to us to get better decisions from our brains, and from the brains of others. That is our mission.

Do we have to use all these ideas? No.

We can choose what feels right for us. We can modify, ignore, and be picky about where we wish to put our attention. Keith's preferences and my preferences will be different than yours. That is okay. We design the path we wish to take in our careers.

So what should we try to do first? Which technique is the most important?

Identify the biggest problem that holds us back. Then, look for ways to get our minds working to fix that problem automatically. If we can remove our biggest frustration, the difference will be huge.

Our minds are powerful. They work 24 hours a day and can take hints and suggestions from us. Let's do our best to be in control of our minds.

Thank you.

Thank you for purchasing and reading this book. We hope you found some ideas that will work for you.

Before you go, would it be okay if we asked a small favor? Would you take just one minute and leave a sentence or two reviewing this book online? Your review can help others choose what they will read next. It would be greatly appreciated by many fellow readers.

More Books from Big Al Books
BigAlBooks.com

Also in the Mindset Series

Secrets to Mastering Your Mindset
Take Control of Your Network Marketing Career

Prospecting and Recruiting Series

How to Get Appointments Without Rejection
Fill Our Calendars with Network Marketing Prospects

Create Influence
10 Ways to Impress and Guide Others

How to Meet New People Guidebook
Overcome Fear and Connect Now

How to Get Your Prospect's Attention and Keep It!
Magic Phrases for Network Marketing

10 Shortcuts Into Our Prospects' Minds
Get Network Marketing Decisions Fast!

How To Prospect, Sell And Build Your Network Marketing Business With Stories

26 Instant Marketing Ideas To Build Your Network Marketing Business

51 Ways and Places to Sponsor New Distributors
Discover Hot Prospects For Your Network Marketing Business

First Sentences for Network Marketing
How To Quickly Get Prospects On Your Side

Big Al's MLM Sponsoring Magic
How To Build A Network Marketing Team Quickly

Start SuperNetworking!
5 Simple Steps to Creating Your Own Personal Networking Group

Getting Started Series

How to Build Your Network Marketing Business in 15 Minutes a Day

3 Easy Habits For Network Marketing
Automate Your MLM Success

Quick Start Guide for Network Marketing
Get Started FAST, Rejection-FREE!

Core Skills Series

How To Get Instant Trust, Belief, Influence and Rapport!
13 Ways To Create Open Minds By Talking To The
Subconscious Mind

Ice Breakers!
How To Get Any Prospect To Beg You For A Presentation

Pre-Closing for Network Marketing
"Yes" Decisions Before The Presentation

The Two-Minute Story for Network Marketing
Create the Big-Picture Story That Sticks!

Personality Training Series (The Colors)

The Four Color Personalities for MLM
The Secret Language for Network Marketing

Mini-Scripts for the Four Color Personalities
How to Talk to our Network Marketing Prospects

Why Are My Goals Not Working?
Color Personalities for Network Marketing Success

How To Get Kids To Say Yes!
Using the Secret Four Color Languages to Get Kids to Listen

Presentation and Closing Series

Closing for Network Marketing
Getting Prospects Across The Finish Line

The One-Minute Presentation
Explain Your Network Marketing Business Like A Pro

How to Follow Up With Your Network Marketing Prospects
Turn Not Now Into Right Now!

Retail Sales for Network Marketers
How to Get New Customers for Your MLM Business

Leadership Series

The Complete Three-Book Network Marketing Leadership Series
Series includes: How To Build Network Marketing Leaders Volume One, How To Build
Network Marketing Leaders Volume Two, and Motivation. Action. Results.

How To Build Network Marketing Leaders
Volume One: Step-By-Step Creation Of MLM Professionals

How To Build Network Marketing Leaders
Volume Two: Activities And Lessons For MLM Leaders

Motivation. Action. Results.
How Network Marketing Leaders Move Their Teams

What Smart Sponsors Do
Supercharge Our Network Marketing Team

More Books...

Why You Need to Start Network Marketing
How to Remove Risk and Have a Better Life

How To Build Your Network Marketing Nutrition Business Fast

How Speakers, Trainers, and Coaches Get More Bookings
12 Ways to Flood Our Calendars with Paid Events

How To Build Your Network Marketing Utilities Business Fast

Getting "Yes" Decisions
What insurance agents and financial advisors can say to clients

Public Speaking Magic
Success and Confidence in the First 20 Seconds

Worthless Sponsor Jokes
Network Marketing Humor

About the Authors

Keith Schreiter has 20+ years of experience in network marketing and MLM. He shows network marketers how to use simple systems to build a stable and growing business.

So, do you need more prospects? Do you need your prospects to commit instead of stalling? Want to know how to engage and keep your group active? If these are the types of skills you would like to master, you will enjoy his "how-to" style.

Keith speaks and trains in the U.S., Canada, and Europe.

Tom "Big Al" Schreiter has 40+ years of experience in network marketing and MLM. As the author of the original "Big Al" training books in the late '70s, he has continued to speak in over 80 countries on using the exact words and phrases to get prospects to open up their minds and say "YES."

His passion is marketing ideas, marketing campaigns, and how to speak to the subconscious mind in simplified, practical ways. He is always looking for case studies of incredible marketing campaigns that give usable lessons.

As the author of numerous audio trainings, Tom is a favorite speaker at company conventions and regional events.